Published by
Balaji

Title: **Pomegranate**

Purchase my books online from:

Amazon

THE AUTHOR
Ji saays

# CONTENT

# Pomegranate Cosmopolitans

## Ingredients

2 cups good vodka (recommended: Grey Goose or Finlandia)

1 cup orange liqueur (recommended: Cointreau)

1 cup cranberry juice cocktail, (recommended: Ocean Spray)

1/2 cup bottled pomegranate juice (recommended: Pom Wonderful)

1/2 cup freshly squeezed lime juice (4 limes)

Thinly sliced limes, for garnish

## Directions

Combine the vodka, orange liqueur, cranberry juice, pomegranate juice, and lime juice in a large pitcher. Fill a cocktail shaker half full with ice, pour the cocktail mixture in, and shake for a full 30 seconds. Pour into martini glasses, garnish with a slice of lime, and serve immediately.

# Pomegranate Lamb

## Ingredients

Marinade and lamb:

Salt and pepper, to taste

8 lamb rib chops, totally trimmed

1 tablespoon rosemary leaves

4 tablespoons pomegranate molasses

4 cloves garlic, thinly sliced

2 bay leaves, broken

1/3 cup virgin olive oil

Garnish: fresh pomegranate seeds, optional

Pomegranate Au jus:

1/2 plus 1/2 tablespoon butter

1 tablespoon olive oil

4 shallots, peeled and chopped fine

4 cloves of garlic, peeled and chopped fine

1 cup pomegranate juice

2 tablespoons red wine vinegar

3 cups rich lamb or chicken stock

Directions

Rub the lamb chops with the salt, pepper and rosemary leaves evenly. Combine all of the remaining ingredients in non-reactive dish. Add the chops and turn over in the mixture a few times. Cover and refrigerate up to four hours ahead of time.

Pomegranate Au jus: Heat a medium sized saucepan on medium heat. Add 1/2 tablespoon of butter and the olive oil. When the butter melts add the shallots and garlic. Allow to cook until lightly cooked, (about 3 minutes), stirring frequently so that the garlic doesn't burn. Now add the pomegranate juice and vinegar. Reduce by half. Add the stock and reduce, skimming as necessary until the sauce will coat the back of a spoon, (about 15 minutes). Remove from the heat and strain the sauce through a fine meshed strainer. Reserve in a small saucepan while you cook the chops.

Heat a grill or grill pan to fairly high heat.

Remove the lamb from the marinade and reason them with a touch of salt and pepper. Grill about four minutes on each side.

Reheat the pomegranate Au jus. When is it just under a boil, whisk in the remaining butter. Divide the sauce between the four plates and center the chops on the sauce. Serve.

## Pomegranate Sangria

Ingredients

1 bottle fruity red wine

2 cups pomegranate juice

1/2 cup brandy

1/2 cup Triple Sec

1/4 cup simple syrup (equal amounts sugar and water, heated until sugar dissolves, cooled)

1/4 cup pomegranate seeds

1 large orange, halved and thinly sliced

1 green apple, cored, halved and thinly sliced

1 cup red grapes, sliced in ½

Directions

Combine all ingredients in a pitcher, cover and refrigerate for at least 4 hours or up to 48 hours before serving. Serve over ice.

## Butternut Squash and Pomegranate Seeds

Ingredients

1 large butternut squash (about 2 1/2 pounds)

2 pounds Brussels sprouts (about 5 cups)

4 red onions, quartered

1/2 cup olive oil

Kosher salt and freshly ground pepper

2 teaspoons chili powder

1/4 cup pomegranate molasses

1 cup pomegranate seeds

Directions

Preheat the oven to 400 degrees F. Use a knife to lop the top and bottom off the squash. Slice the skin off the sides, then cut the squash in half lengthwise and remove the seeds. Chop into small pieces. Divide the squash between 2 baking sheets.

Trim the Brussels sprouts, then cut them in half if desired (or you can leave them whole). Arrange on the baking sheets with the squash. Break the quartered onions apart and add them to the baking sheets.

Drizzle the vegetables with the olive oil. Season with salt and pepper, sprinkle with the chili powder and toss. Roast 30 to 35 minutes, or until browned.

Take the vegetables out of the oven and tip into a serving dish. Drizzle with the pomegranate molasses and sprinkle on the pomegranate seeds. Toss and serve immediately.

## Pomegranate Gelatin

Ingredients

2 cups pomegranate juice, not from concentrate

2 envelopes unflavored gelatin

2 tablespoons sugar

1/2 cup pomegranate seeds

Directions

Place 1/2 cup of the pomegranate juice into a medium mixing bowl and sprinkle the gelatin on top. Set aside.

Place the remaining juice and the sugar into a small saucepan and place over high heat. Bring just to a boil. Remove from the heat and add to the juice and gelatin mixture, stirring to combine. Place the bowl into the refrigerator and chill, just until the mixture begins to set up, approximately 30 to 40 minutes. Remove from the refrigerator and stir in the seeds. Place into a 2 cup mold of your choice or 4 1/2 cup individual molds and chill until set.

## Pomegranate Maple Syrup

Ingredients

1 cup pomegranate juice

1 small sprig fresh rosemary

1/2 cup maple syrup

Directions

Combine the pomegranate juice and rosemary sprig in a small saucepan and bring to a simmer over medium heat. Simmer until reduced by three-quarters and syrupy, 10 to 15 minutes. Remove from the heat and stir in the maple syrup; strain.

## Cheesecake with Pomegranate Sauce

Ingredients

Crust:

5 tablespoons unsalted butter, melted and cooled, plus more for buttering the pan

12 graham crackers

1/4 cup granulated sugar

1/4 teaspoon salt

Filling:

Four 8-ounce packages cream cheese, at room temperature

1 1/4 cups granulated sugar

1/2 teaspoon vanilla extract

4 large eggs

1/2 cup sour cream

Pomegranate Sauce:

2 cups pomegranate juice

1/4 cup granulated sugar

1/2 cup fresh pomegranate seeds

Directions

For the crust: Preheat the oven to 350 degrees F. Wrap 3 layers of foil around the outside of a 9-inch-diameter springform pan with 3-inch-high sides. Butter the pan.

Combine the graham crackers, sugar and salt in a food processor and pulse until crumbly. Add the butter and pulse until moistened. Press the crumb mixture evenly onto the bottom and 1 1/2 inches up the sides of the prepared pan. Bake just until golden brown, about 15 minutes. Let cool completely.

Reduce the oven temperature to 325 degrees F.

For the filling: In an electric mixer fitted with the paddle attachment, beat the cream cheese on medium speed until fluffy. Add the sugar and vanilla and beat until combined. Add the eggs 1 at a time, mixing well after each addition. Add the sour cream and mix until smooth, about 35 seconds. Pour the filling into the cooled crust.

Set the cheesecake in a large baking pan. Add enough hot water to the baking pan to come 1 inch up the sides of the cheesecake pan. Bake until almost set (the center will move slightly when the pan is gently shaken) but not puffed, about 1 hour. Let cool at room temperature for 2 hours. Cover loosely with plastic wrap and refrigerate until completely cooled, preferably overnight or for at least 6 hours.

For the pomegranate sauce: Combine the pomegranate juice and sugar in a saucepan and cook over high heat until reduced to 1/2 cup, about 15 minutes. Let cool. Add the pomegranate seeds and mix to combine.

Pour the pomegranate sauce on top of the cooled cheesecake and serve.

# Pomegranate, Arugula Salad

## Ingredients

1/4 cup pomegranate molasses

1/2 lemon, juiced

2 tablespoons honey

2 tablespoons red wine vinegar

3/4 cup olive oil

Kosher salt and freshly ground black pepper

6 cups lightly packed arugula, leafy hydroponic - if available

1 pomegranate, seeds only

1/4 cup Parmigiano-Reggiano shavings

1/4 cup toasted walnuts

1 shallot, sliced

## Directions

To make vinaigrette, combine molasses, lemon juice, honey and vinegar in a mixing bowl and whisk to combine. Slowly drizzle in olive oil while you whisk to emulsify. Season, to taste, with salt and pepper.

Toss salad ingredients together and dress with the vinaigrette.

# Pomegranate Quinoa Pilaf

## Ingredients

2 tablespoons olive oil

1/2 medium onion, diced

1 cup quinoa

2 cups low-sodium chicken broth

1/2 cup pomegranate seeds

1/2 cup diagonally sliced scallions

1 tablespoon chopped fresh flat-leaf parsley

Juice of 1/2 lemon

1 teaspoon fresh lemon zest

1 teaspoon sugar

Salt and freshly ground black pepper

1/2 cup slivered almonds, toasted


Directions


Heat 1 tablespoon olive oil in a heavy-bottomed saucepan over medium-high heat. Saute the onion until translucent and fragrant. Add the quinoa and stir to coat. Add the chicken broth and bring to a boil. Lower the heat and simmer for about 20 minutes, until the liquid is absorbed and the quinoa is tender.


In a large mixing bowl, combine 1 tablespoon olive oil, pomegranate seeds, scallions, parsley, lemon juice, zest, and sugar. Add the quinoa and season with salt, and pepper to taste. Garnish with toasted, slivered almonds.


## Pomegranate Guacamole


Ingredients


1/2 small white onion, finely chopped

1 serrano chile, finely diced

3 ripe avocados

1/4 cup finely chopped fresh cilantro

1 1/4 teaspoons kosher salt

Juice of 2 limes

1 large clove garlic, minced

Seeds from 1/2 medium pomegranate (about 1/2 cup)

Directions

In a medium bowl add the onion and the chile. Split the avocados in half and remove the pits. Scoop the avocados into the bowl along with the cilantro, salt, lime juice and garlic. Mash everything together, and then fold in the pomegranate seeds.

## Pomegranate Holiday Salad

Ingredients

4 cups arugula

3 tablespoons chopped toasted walnuts

1 fennel bulb, thinly sliced, plus 1 tablespoon chopped fronds, for garnish

1 orange, segmented, plus the juice squeezed from the pulp

Seeds from 1 pomegranate

1/2 red onion, thinly sliced

1 tablespoon Dijon mustard

1 tablespoon balsamic vinegar

3 tablespoons extra-virgin olive oil

Salt and freshly ground black pepper

Directions

Toss the arugula, walnuts, fennel, orange segments, pomegranate seeds and onions together in a large bowl.

Whisk together the Dijon, vinegar and orange juice in a small bowl. Whisk in the oil. Season with salt and pepper.

Drizzle the salad with the dressing to taste. Garnish with fennel fronds and serve immediately.

## Pomegranate Spritz Cookies

Ingredients

2 cups all-purpose flour

1/2 teaspoon baking powder

1/4 teaspoon salt

10 tablespoons unsalted butter, at room temperature

2/3 cup sugar

1 large egg

2 tablespoons pomegranate molasses

3/4 teaspoon red food coloring

1/2 teaspoon finely grated orange zest

Silver nonpareils, for decorating

Directions

Position racks in the upper and lower thirds of the oven and preheat to 300 degrees F. Whisk the flour, baking powder and salt in a medium bowl. Beat the butter and sugar in a large bowl with a mixer on medium-high speed until light and fluffy, about 3 minutes. Beat in the egg, pomegranate molasses, food coloring and orange zest. Reduce the mixer speed to medium low; beat in the flour mixture until incorporated. (The dough can be made a day ahead; cover and refrigerate. Bring to room temperature before filling your cookie press.)

Fill a cookie press with the dough according to the manufacturer's instructions. Press cookies 1 inch apart onto 2 baking sheets. Decorate with nonpareils.

Bake, switching the pans halfway through, until the cookies are set but not browned, 15 to 18 minutes. Let cool 5 minutes on the baking sheets, loosen with a thin spatula and let cool completely on the baking sheets. Repeat with the remaining dough.

# Cranberry Pomegranate Crumb Bars

Ingredients

Crust:

2 cups pecans

4 sticks (2 cups) unsalted butter, softened, plus more for the pan

4 cups all-purpose flour

2 cups granulated sugar

1/2 teaspoon kosher salt

Filling:

1 cup pomegranate juice

2 tablespoons cornstarch

1 pound fresh or thawed frozen cranberries

1 cup granulated sugar

2 teaspoons finely grated orange zest

Confectioners' sugar, for dusting

Ground cinnamon, for dusting

Directions

For the crust: Preheat the oven to 375 degrees F.

Spread the pecans on a rimmed baking pan and bake until lightly toasted, about 4 minutes. Cool completely.

Butter a 9-by-13-inch baking pan, then line it with parchment paper, leaving a 2-inch overhang on 2 sides; butter the parchment and sides of the pan.

To make the shortbread crust: Pulse the pecans in a food processor until finely ground. Transfer to the bowl of a stand mixer fitted with the paddle attachment. Add the flour and mix on low speed to combine. Add the granulated sugar, salt and butter and mix on medium speed until the dough comes together, scraping down the sides of the bowl as needed. Remove 2 cups of the dough and reserve. Turn the remaining dough out into the prepared baking pan and press evenly into the bottom of the pan. Dock the dough all over with a fork.

Bake until light golden brown, about 20 minutes. Set on a cooling rack to cool completely, about 30 minutes. Keep the oven on.

For the filling: Put 1/4 cup of the pomegranate juice in a small bowl and stir in the cornstarch; set aside. Combine the cranberries, granulated sugar, orange zest and remaining 3/4 cup pomegranate juice in a medium saucepan. Bring to a brisk simmer over medium-high heat and simmer, lightly mashing the cranberries, until some of the liquid has reduced and the cranberries are just starting to soften, 5 to 8 minutes. Add the cornstarch mixture and simmer until thickened, 1 to 2 minutes. Pour into a bowl and submerge the bowl into a larger bowl of ice water to cool, about 10 minutes.

Pour the cooled filling over the crust and spread it evenly. Crumble the reserved dough evenly over the top, then bake until the filling is bubbling and the crumbs are golden brown, 30 to 35 minutes. Cool completely in the pan, about 30 minutes.

Dust generously with confectioners' sugar and cinnamon. Remove from the pan, trim the edges if desired and cut into squares.

## Pomegranate-Cinnamon Grilled Quail

Ingredients

1/2 cup pomegranate molasses

2 tablespoons fresh orange juice

1 teaspoon ground cinnamon

8 quail, butterflied

Canola oil, for drizzling

Salt and freshly ground black pepper

Directions

Heat grill to medium. Combine pomegranate molasses, orange juice, and cinnamon in a small bowl. Drizzle quail with canola oil and season with salt and pepper. Grill, breast-side down, over medium heat, for about 7 minutes total or until golden brown and slightly charred. When quail is 3/4 cooked brush with glaze, turn over, brush the other side with glaze, and continue grilling until just cooked through. Remove from the grill and serve 2 quail per person.

## Lamb Kebabs with Pomegranate Glaze

Ingredients

Lamb Kebabs:

1 pound ground lamb

3 quarter-size slices ginger

2 large cloves garlic or 4 small

2 medium shallots

Zest of 1 lemon, and separately, its juice

4 sprigs fresh mint

Handful fresh cilantro

3/4 teaspoon kosher salt

4 tablespoons pomegranate molasses

1/2 teaspoon baking soda

1/4 teaspoon garam masala, optional

Lots of freshly ground pepper

Oil, for drizzling

Cucumber Raita:

1 cup plain yogurt

2 tablespoons minced fresh mint

1 large English cucumber, grated

1 clove garlic, minced

Kosher salt and freshly ground pepper

Directions

Special equipment: Food processor if you have it, 8 bamboo skewers, stovetop griddle or big nonstick pan or outside grill

For the lamb: Bring the lamb to room temperature. If you're going to cook your kebabs on the grill, soak bamboo skewers in water for at least 30 minutes, so they don't burn. Grab your food processor. You can chop all this by hand too; just make sure to chop it all up very finely. Throw the ginger, garlic, shallots, lemon zest, mint, cilantro and salt into the processor. Grind until very finely chopped. Throw the lamb into a big bowl. Add the shallot mixture, 2 tablespoons pomegranate molasses, baking soda, garam masala if using and pepper to the meat. Using your hands, knead 2 to 5 minutes until the meat lightens in color, taking on the appearance of knitted fabric. It will also be very sticky. Perfect! Divide the meat in half, then in half again and then half again, until you have 8 mounds. Have a platter ready for your completed kebabs. Drizzle a little oil on the platter so the kebabs don't stick. Have your bamboo skewers standing by. Take one ball of meat and roll it into a short stump. Thread the skewer through it, and then begin shaping the kebab with quick strokes, pulling the meat down. It should be a little over 1/4-inch thick. Roll the kebab between your hands to seal the meat. Repeat. Preheat a griddle over medium heat, drizzling oil over it, so that when it starts to smoke, you'll know it's ready. Meanwhile, mix the juice of half the lemon with the remaining 2 tablespoons pomegranate molasses in a small bowl. When it's hot, place the skewers on the grill. Cook about 2 minutes, then turn a quarter of the way. Brush with the lemon-molasses glaze and cook another 2 minutes. Continue in this way until you've cooked the meat 8 to 10 minutes.

For the raita: Mix the yogurt, mint, cucumber and garlic together. Season with salt and pepper, and serve alongside the kebabs.

## Grilled Leg of Lamb with Pomegranate Molasses

Ingredients

4 to 5-pound boneless leg of lamb, rolled and tied

1/2 cup pomegranate molasses, plus extra for serving, store-bought or recipe follows

Kosher salt and freshly ground black pepper to taste

Pomegranate Syrup or Molasses:

4 cups pomegranate juice

1/2 cup sugar

1 tablespoon freshly squeezed lemon juice

Directions

Preheat the grill to 375 degrees F.

Unroll the lamb and brush on all sides with the molasses. Season on all sides with salt and pepper. Roll the lamb up and secure with butchers' twine. Place the lamb over indirect heat and cook for 15 minutes, brush with the molasses again. Turn 1/4 turn and cook for another 15 minutes. Complete the brushing and turning procedure 2 more times for a total cooking time of approximately 1 hour or until the lamb reaches an internal temperature of 130 degrees F. Remove from the heat and allow to rest 10 minutes before slicing and serving. Serve with additional molasses if desired.

Pomegranate Syrup or Molasses:

For Syrup: Place the pomegranate juice, sugar and lemon juice in a 4-quart saucepan set over medium heat. Cook, stirring occasionally, until the sugar has completely dissolved. Once the sugar has dissolved, reduce the heat to medium-low and cook until the mixture has reduced to 1 1/2 cups, approximately 50 minutes. It should be the consistency of syrup. Remove from the heat and allow to cool in the saucepan for 30 minutes. Transfer to a glass jar and allow to cool completely before covering and storing in the refrigerator for up to 6 months.

For Molasses: Place the pomegranate juice, sugar and lemon juice in a 4-quart saucepan set over medium heat. Cook, stirring occasionally, until the sugar has completely dissolved. Once the sugar has dissolved, reduce the heat to medium-low and cook until the mixture has reduced to 1 cup, approximately 70 minutes. It should be the consistency of thick syrup. Remove from the heat and allow to cool in the saucepan for 30 minutes. Transfer to a glass jar and allow to cool completely before covering and storing in the refrigerator for up to 6 months.

# Cornish Game Hens with Pomegranate Molasses

## Ingredients

4 Cornish game hens, split, spine and wing tips removed

Extra-virgin olive oil

Kosher salt

1 bottle (12 fluid ounces) pomegranate molasses

2 cloves garlic, smashed

1/2 cup chicken stock

2 tablespoons sliced scallion greens, cut thin on the bias, for garnish

## Directions

Preheat the oven to 350 degrees F.

Tie each hen's legs together with butcher's twine or a blanched scallion green.

Coat a large saute pan with olive oil and bring to medium-high heat. Season the hens on both sides generously with salt. Carefully lay the hens in the pan, skin side down, and cook until the skin becomes brown and crispy, 6 to 7 minutes. Turn the hens over and brown on the flesh side. Do not crowd your pan, you may need to do this in batches. Remove the hens to a sheet tray.

Meanwhile, combine the molasses and garlic in a saucepan over medium heat. Bring the molasses to a boil and reduce by half until syrupy, about 20 minutes.

Brush the hens on both sides with the reduced molasses. Put the hens in the oven and roast until they are cooked through, basting occasionally, about 20 minutes.

Remove the hens from the oven and garnish with the sliced scallions.

## Roasted Quail Date and Pomegranate Marinade

Ingredients

4 quails

1 small onion, finely diced

1/4 cup diced celery

1 small garlic clove, diced

1/2 cup date syrup

1/2 cup pomegranate syrup

1/2 cup red wine

1/4 cup honey

1/4 teaspoon cumin powder

1/4 teaspoon anise seed

1/4 teaspoon sumac

1/4 teaspoon coriander powder

1 tablespoon extra-virgin olive oil

Pomegranate seeds, fresh

Parsley leaves, or basil chiffonade


Directions


Remove the backbones from the quail or ask your butcher to do this for you. Rinse and dry them on paper towels. Place in a shallow pan. Mix remaining ingredients, except pomegranate seeds and parsley, in a large bowl. Pour mixture over the quail and refrigerate for 30 minutes to 1 hour.


Preheat oven to 450 degrees F.


Drain the quail and keep the marinade. Place the quail in a roasting pan with some olive oil and roast them for 15 minutes or until done. Meanwhile, strain the marinade into a pot and bring it to a boil. Reduce the heat and cook until syrupy. You may wish to add 1 teaspoon of butter or olive oil. Mix well. Taste the marinade and season, to taste.

Pour the sauce onto 4 plates and place the roasted quail on top. Garnish with pomegranate seeds and parsley.

## Duck Breast with Apple-Pomegranate Sauce

Ingredients

Duck:

1 tablespoon grapeseed oil

2 duck breasts, skin on

1 teaspoon curry powder

Salt

Sauce:

3 tablespoons unsalted butter, at room temperature, divided

1/4 cup pomegranate juice

1 Pink Lady apple (or other crisp, firm apple) peeled, cored, and finely diced

1/4 onion, finely diced

Pinch sugar, if needed

Mashed Sweet Potatoes with Goat Cheese, for serving, recipe follows

Sauteed Julienned Vegetables, for serving, recipe follows

Mashed Sweet Potatoes with Goat Cheese:

2 large sweet potatoes

Salt

2 tablespoons goat cheese

1 tablespoon honey

Pinch ground ginger

Pinch ground cinnamon

1 teaspoon unsalted butter

Sauteed Julienned Vegetables:

Grapeseed oil

2 carrots, peeled and julienned

1/4 pound snow peas, julienned

1 small daikon, julienned

Salt and freshly ground black pepper

Directions

Sauce:

Heat a medium saute pan over medium-high heat and add the oil.

Cut a crosshatch pattern into the skin of the duck breasts. Be careful to not cut through to the flesh.

Season the skin side with the curry and the flesh side with salt. Place in the pan, skin side down. Cook on the skin side to render of some of the fat and crisp up the skin, 5 to 7 minutes. Once the skin is crisp, flip the breasts, reduce the heat to medium, and cook on the flesh side for about 4 minutes for medium-rare. Once cooked, remove from the pan and allow the meat to rest for 5 minutes.

Make the sauce in the same pan used for the duck. (Wipe out the pan if you have burned bits on the bottom, and add some butter.) Place the pan over medium-high heat and add 1 tablespoon butter. Deglaze the pan with the pomegranate juice. Allow the juice to simmer and reduce by half. Turn off the heat and stir in the remaining 2 tablespoons butter. Taste and season with a pinch of sugar if the sauce tastes too tart.

When plating, slice the duck breast thinly and spoon the warm sauce over the duck. Serve with Mashed Sweet Potatoes with Goat Cheese and Sauteed Julienned Vegetables.

Mashed Sweet Potatoes with Goat Cheese:

Peel and slice the sweet potatoes into 1/2-inch pieces. Place the potatoes in a large saucepan, fill with water to cover the potatoes, and add some salt. Bring the water to a boil over medium-high heat. Cook the potatoes until fork tender, about 13 minutes. Stick a fork in a potato piece and if it goes in easily, it's done.

Drain the potatoes well. Transfer them to a food processor and blend until smooth. Add the goat cheese, honey, ginger, cinnamon, butter, and 1/2 teaspoon salt. Blend again until everything is well combined. Transfer to a bowl and let cool for 1 minute.

Spoon the potatoes into a zip-top plastic bag or a pastry bag with a tip for piping, or spoon directly onto plates. If piping, cut a hole in the tip and pipe onto the plate.

Sauteed Julienned Vegetables:

Heat a saute pan over medium heat and add some oil. Saute the julienned vegetables and season with salt and pepper. Cook until the vegetables are just softened, 3 to 5 minutes. Taste a bite and cook for another minute if the vegetables are still hard.

## Roasted Brussels sprouts With Pomegranate and Hazelnuts

Ingredients

1 1/4 pounds Brussels sprouts, trimmed and halved

2 tablespoons canola oil

Kosher salt and freshly ground pepper

3 tablespoons pomegranate molasses

Seeds from 1 pomegranate

1/2 cup coarsely chopped toasted hazelnuts

Finely grated zest of 1 lime

1 tablespoon finely grated orange zest

Directions

Preheat the oven to 375 degrees F.

Put the Brussels sprouts in a medium roasting pan; toss with the canola oil and season with salt and pepper. Roast in the oven until light golden brown and a knife inserted into the centers goes in without any resistance, about 45 minutes.

Transfer the sprouts to a large bowl and add the pomegranate molasses, pomegranate seeds, hazelnuts, and lime and orange zests. Season with salt as needed.

## Lamb Chops with Pomegranate Sauce and Saffron Pilaf

Ingredients

2 tablespoons butter

1/4 cup orzo pasta

1 cup white rice

2 pinches saffron threads

1 3/4 cups chicken stock

1 to 2 large pomegranates or 1 cup store-bought pomegranate juice

1/2 cup red wine

2 tablespoons Worcestershire sauce

6 peppercorns

3 whole cloves

1 fresh bay leaf

1 1/2 tablespoons cornstarch

12 rib lamb chops

Salt and freshly ground black pepper

2 tablespoons extra-virgin olive oil

2 large garlic cloves, chopped

1 pound farm spinach (available in bundles rather than bags in produce section), washed and dried

Freshly grated nutmeg

Directions

Preheat the broiler and arrange the oven rack 8 inches from the broiler.

Heat a large sauce pot over medium heat. Add the butter and let it melt, then add the orzo and stir. Toast the pasta until golden brown, 3 minutes, then add the rice and stir to combine. Add the saffron threads and stir in the stock. Bring the liquid to a boil, then reduce the heat to a simmer and cover the pot with a tight-fitting lid. Cook the rice until tender, about 15 to 18 minutes.

Meanwhile, roll the pomegranate on the counter while applying pressure for a minute. Hold the pomegranate over a small pot and cut into it with a small sharp knife; the juice will come rushing out. Squeeze the pomegranate until 3/4 to 1 cup of juice is produced. Stir in the wine, Worcestershire, peppercorns, cloves, and bay leaf. Bring to a boil, lower the heat to a simmer and reduce the liquid by half, about 6 minutes. Pour a little sauce into a small bowl, stir in the cornstarch, and then pour the mixture into the sauce. Cook until thickened, about 1 minute. Remove and discard the peppercorns, whole cloves and the bay leaf.

Arrange the chops on a broiler pan and season with salt and pepper, to taste. Broil for 3 to 4 minutes, or only 1 minute on each side for pink centers.

When the chops go into the broiler, heat the extra-virgin olive oil in a medium skillet over medium heat. Add the garlic and stir for 2 minutes, then add the spinach and let it wilt. Season with salt, pepper, and nutmeg, to taste.

Arrange 3 chops on each serving plate. Drizzle with pomegranate sauce, and serve the saffron pilaf and wilted spinach alongside.

## Black Pepper-Pomegranate Molasses Glazed Turkey

Ingredients

For the glaze:

1 1/2 cups pomegranate molasses

3/4 cup prepared horseradish, drained

3 tablespoons Dijon mustard

Kosher salt and freshly ground pepper

For the turkey:

1 15-pound fresh turkey

1 stick unsalted butter, softened

Kosher salt and freshly ground pepper

4 cups homemade chicken stock or low-sodium canned broth, warmed

## Directions

Preheat the oven to 450 degrees F. Make the glaze: Whisk the pomegranate molasses, horseradish, mustard, 1/2 teaspoon salt and 1 1/2 teaspoons pepper in a medium bowl. Let it sit at room temperature to allow the flavors to meld.

Meanwhile, prepare the turkey: Remove the neck and giblets, then rinse the bird inside and out with cold water and pat dry. Rub the entire surface of the bird with the butter and season well (including inside the cavity) with salt and pepper. Truss the turkey with kitchen twine and place it breast-side up on a rack in a large roasting pan. Roast until slightly golden brown, about 45 minutes.

Reduce the oven temperature to 350 degrees F and continue roasting 1 more hour, basting with the chicken stock every 15 minutes. Brush the entire turkey with 1 cup of the pomegranate glaze and continue roasting until an instant-read thermometer inserted into the thigh registers 160 degrees F, about 15 more minutes.

Remove the turkey from the oven and brush with the remaining glaze. Tent loosely with foil and let sit 15 minutes before carving.

## Blueberry-Pomegranate Power Bowl with Toasted Quinoa Croutons

## Ingredients

Toasted Quinoa Croutons:

Nonstick spray

1 cup old-fashioned rolled oats, such as Bob's Red Mill

3/4 cup quinoa

1/2 cup slivered almonds

1/2 cup pumpkin seeds

Large pinch kosher salt

1/2 to 2/3 cup coconut oil, melted

2 tablespoons agave syrup

Power Bowl:

1 cup old-fashioned rolled oats, such as Bob's Red Mill

2 cups frozen organic wild blueberries, plus a few extra for garnish

1 frozen banana, halved

1 cup nonfat Greek yogurt, plus 1/4 cup for garnish

3/4 cup pomegranate juice

2 tablespoons honey

2 tablespoons pomegranate molasses

Juice of 1/2 lemon

2 teaspoons freshly grated orange zest

Pomegranate seeds, for garnish, optional


Directions


For the croutons: Preheat the oven to 300 degrees F. Line a 9-by-13-inch baking sheet with parchment paper, and spray with nonstick spray.


Toss the oats with the quinoa, almonds, pumpkin seeds and salt in a large bowl. Add 1/2 cup coconut oil (if it has hardened in the jar, melt it in the microwave or on the stove over low heat) and agave. Toss until the mixture forms clumps; if it seems dry, add more coconut oil, 1 tablespoon at a time.


Spread the crouton mixture onto the prepared baking sheet in a thin, even layer. Bake on the middle oven rack until light golden brown, about 45 minutes--it will feel sticky when just out of the oven but will crisp up as it cools.


Remove the baking sheet to a baking rack and let cool completely. Break into clusters. (Makes about 3 cups. Extra can be stored at room temperature in a tightly covered container for 3 days.)

For the power bowl: Put the oats in a blender and blend until powder-like. Add the blueberries, banana, yogurt, pomegranate juice, honey, pomegranate molasses, lemon juice and orange zest. Blend until smooth.

Transfer the mixture to a container with a tight-fitting lid and refrigerate for at least 8 hour and up to 24 hours. (This will help create a smoother consistency as the oats will absorb some of the liquid and become thicker.)

To serve, divide the power bowl mixture between 2 bowls. Top with a dollop of yogurt, a few blueberries, some pomegranate seeds if using, and some quinoa croutons.

## Barley and Wild Rice Pilaf with Pomegranate Seeds

Ingredients

2 teaspoons extra-virgin olive oil

1 medium onion, finely chopped

1/2 cup wild rice, rinsed

1/2 cup pearl barley

3 cups reduced-sodium chicken broth or vegetable broth

1/3 cup pine nuts

1 cup pomegranate seeds (1 large fruit; see Tip)

2 teaspoons freshly grated lemon zest

2 tablespoons chopped flat-leaf parsley

Directions

Heat oil in a large saucepan over medium heat. Add onion and cook, stirring often, until softened. Add wild rice and barley; stir for a few seconds. Add broth and bring to a simmer. Reduce heat to low, cover and simmer until the wild rice and barley are tender and most of the liquid has been absorbed, 45 to 50 minutes.

Meanwhile, toast pine nuts in a small, dry skillet over medium-low heat, stirring constantly, until light golden and fragrant, 2 to 3 minutes. Transfer to a small bowl to cool.

Add pomegranate seeds, lemon zest, parsley and the toasted pine nuts to the pilaf; fluff with a fork. Serve hot.

## Pomegranate, Sriracha and Mint Chicken Wings

Ingredients

Wings:

2 pounds chicken wings

2 tablespoons coriander seeds

1 generous tablespoon cumin seeds

1 generous tablespoon cracked black peppercorns

Seeds of 16 green cardamom pods, or 1/2 teaspoon cardamom seeds

2 tablespoons dry mustard

1 generous tablespoon salt

Nonstick spray or canola oil

Sauce:

3 tablespoons grapeseed or canola oil

8 cloves garlic, smashed

1/4 cup pomegranate molasses*

1 1/2 tablespoons Sriracha (Thai chili sauce; use more if you like it spicy!)

1 small bunch fresh mint, leaves picked

4 tablespoons (1/2 stick) butter

2 teaspoons lemon juice

Kosher salt and freshly ground black pepper

Directions

For the wings: Pat the chicken wings dry with a paper towel; don't skip this step! This will both help the rub adhere and ensure crispy skin.

To a spice grinder or mortar and pestle, add the coriander seeds, cumin seeds, cracked black peppercorns and cardamom seeds. Grind it to a fine powder.

Pour the ground spice mixture into a small bowl and add the mustard and salt. Whisk to combine. Reserve a scant 2 tablespoons of this mixture for the sauce.

Place the wings in a large bowl and add remaining spice mixture; toss to coat the wings well. Let those puppies sit for about an hour.

About 15 minutes before you're ready to bake, preheat your oven to 375 degrees F. Line a baking sheet with a wire rack and grease with cooking spray (or brush with canola oil).

Place the wings on the prepared rack at an even distance from each other. Pop into the oven for about 45 minutes, flipping the wings over halfway through, and rotating the baking sheet for even cooking.

As the wings are roasting away, make the sauce: In a small saucepan over medium heat, warm the grapeseed oil until shimmering. Add the garlic and cook for about 30 seconds. Then add the reserved 2 tablespoons spice blend and cook another 30 seconds. Stir in the pomegranate molasses, Sriracha and mint leaves. Cook for about 5 minutes, and then finish with the butter and lemon juice. Stir, taste for seasoning and set aside off the heat.

When the wings are done, pull the garlic cloves and mint out of the glaze and discard (thin the sauce with a few teaspoon of water if needed). Toss the wings with the sauce. Avoid the temptation to eat them all yourself! Serve.

Printed in Great Britain
by Amazon

15234779R00018